FLIES OF THE SOUTHWEST

For Lakes (& Streams)

Mike Yeager

Dedicated to
T.R.
For all the times we didn't go fishing.

Photography: Mike Yeager
Illustrations: Lisa Yeager
Fly plates photographed by: Jim Schollmeyer
Book Design: Amy Tomlinson
Softbound ISBN: 1-57188-178-6   Softbound UPC: 0-66066-00380-5

Frank Amato Publications, Inc.
P.O. Box 82112, Portland, Oregon 97282
(503) 653-8108

Printed in Winnipeg, Canada
1 3 5 7 9 10 8 6 4 2

FLIES OF THE

Southwest

For Lakes (& Streams)

Mike Yeager

Frank Amato
PORTLAND

ACKNOWLEDGMENTS

I have fished for many years and must acknowledge here those people, besides my parents, who are most responsible for my participation in the rewarding sport of fly fishing.

My old friend Bob Kirkpatrick got me into his boat on Sunrise Lake in October 1985 and aroused my curiosity in this effective way to catch trout. Kirk and I rode many miles together in our careers with the State of Arizona. These escapades would fill another book on how men work and play hard.

My family, especially my wife Grace, has been a constant source of encouragement in carrying on the sport of fly fishing and in putting this book together. Grace made sure I had a Buck's Bag under the Christmas tree in 1989. She continues to believe that I can do anything.

Joe Clifford has been another source of inspiration. Joe and I try to spend a week or two each September on a low-budget trip to one of the fly fishing Meccas of the West. We have visited such renowned places as Yellowstone Park, the Green River, and the San Juan River in past years. Joe grew up in McNary, Arizona and fished much of the Fort Apache Indian Reservation before many of today's roads were there. He now is a water-rights attorney for the State of Arizona's Attorney General's Office.

A special thanks is due Lyle Worman, owner and operator of Pinetop Sporting Goods in Pinetop, Arizona. Lyle made me a much better fly tier through his orders for several hundred dozens of flies in myriad patterns over the past five years.

Other acknowledgments must include John McKim, Jack Dennis, Terry Hellekson, Randall Kaufmann, Don Puterbaugh, Paul Fling, Eric Leiser, and Lefty Kreh. These authors, fly fishers, and fly tiers have taught me many of the basics and the subtleties of both fly fishing and fly tying.

Dale Clemens and Skip Morris have both contributed greatly to my knowledge of how to construct my fly rods. Without their expert guidance I might be fishing with a willow switch. Deke Meyer has assisted in the efforts to teach this old dog a new trick; the art of fishing from a float tube.

There are many other contributors who have helped me progress in this sport. It is very gratifying to know that such expertise is available within the covers of their many fine publications.

CONTENTS

PREFACE

It has long been a dream of mine to write a book on fly fishing. My affair with fly fishing began several months after the death of my youngest son in 1985. I was invited by an old friend to fly fish Sunrise Lake on the Fort Apache Indian Reservation. It was the diversion I needed to get back on track and get on with my life.

I have fished since I was old enough to hold a pole. My parents were good that way. The first fish I remember catching was a freshwater drum, caught on a worm from a man-made canal near Milan, Illinois. The year was around 1943. My two brothers and I grew up in that humid part of the country. We explored the Mississippi River and its tributaries the Rock River, the Green River, the Edwards River, the Hennipen Canal, and Mill Creek where we used to seine our bait.

My parents gave me my first fly rod and reel when I graduated from grammar school in 1952. Those treasures I still have today. That old three-piece South Bend split bamboo rod and the Oren-o-matic automatic reel saw considerable action and caught many bluegill sunfish, crappies, and other panfish. I didn't fly fish so much as I fished with a fly rod. The deadly "fly" of choice consisted of a small Junebug or Colorado spinner, with a long-shanked size 12 hook loaded with garden hackle. Usually some sort of float was used to secure the proper depth of the "fly." It truly was a deadly combination for catching the warmwater panfish of that area. It also allowed a boy from a family of moderate means to participate in a sport that had a reputation for being that of the elite.

That old fly rod saw a great deal of action in those Midwestern waters until I left there to attend the University of Arizona in Tucson in 1956. The fly rod stayed behind as, at the age of 18, I ventured into the unknown on a new life at a major university, half way across the country. After nearly flunking out the first semester, I finally figured out what study habits were, and four years later I received my degree in Wildlife Management.

Sometime, somehow that old fly rod caught up with me in Arizona. I don't remember how it got here but it remains a cherished old friend with which I can share many angling memories of years passed.

During a 30-plus-year career in wildlife conservation work with the State of Arizona, I managed to log a great deal of fishing time. My trips ranged from the Colorado River at Yuma, to lakes Havasu, Alamo, and Mead, to Lees Ferry and Lake Powell. They included the Verde River and Salt River chains of lakes and the high-country lakes from Flagstaff to the Mogollon Rim into the White Mountains. There was also considerable vacation time spent on the Sea of Cortez. There was also time spent finding the way to Rosecrans Street in San Diego so as not to miss the albacore boat. Most of these trips were low-budget affairs with multiple bodies; car-pooling and equipment sharing being the rule.

A person tends to fish the waters closest to home while the frequency of visits to more distant waters decreases with their distance from home. Through the years spent fishing, bait, plugs, spinners (usually very large), lead-headed jigs, spinning rods, and reels etc., were the method of choice both in and out of Arizona.

My family and I moved to the White Mountain area of Arizona in September of 1977. While an occasional trip to Mexico or a jaunt to Lake Mead or Lees Ferry was still in order, my fishing activities slowed considerably after moving to Lakeside.

In early December 1984, my youngest son was diagnosed with bone cancer. T. R. passed away in early May 1985, five months short of his 19th birthday.

After the funeral, when everyone else had gone, the full impact of losing one of my children really set in on my wife, daughter, and myself. It was more than six weeks later when I finally returned to work.

By the time early October rolled around I was ready to greet an old friend. I hadn't seen Kirk in several years but was glad to take him up on his invitation to again fish with a fly rod. I was assured that this time however, we would use real hand-tied flies.

This fishing was done from a boat, which was usually anchored while casting and stripping the fly line. The fish would take the fly at various stages of the retrieve and usually put up a good tussle in the landing process. The day was clear, the company was excellent, and the colors of autumn in Arizona's high country were breathtaking. The events of that day have lingered with me over the past 12 years. This book will attempt to reveal to the reader some of the techniques I began to learn about lake fly fishing on Sunrise Lake in October 1985.

I continue to learn how to enjoy this highly successful method of fishing while maintaining the low-budget approach that has allowed me to sustain in my sport.

INTRODUCTION

John Merwin's fine book *Stillwater Trout* is introduced as follows: "Ponds and lakes are the poor sisters of American trout waters." It is sad that so fine a writer can introduce such a fine publication with such a misguided statement. If lakes and ponds are the poor sisters, then it would seem to follow

Joe Clifford with a rainbow caught at Stone Lake, New Mexico.

that those who fish lakes regularly might be classed at the least as indi-gents. This creates an interesting dilemma: I fly fish both streams and lakes/ponds and I have yet to feel like I have denigrated myself by fishing one or the other. I am not transformed into something different when I go from lake to stream and back again. What does happen is that some of the tactics and equipment change. I greatly enjoy both types of fishing but tend to favor lake and pond fishing because I consistently have better success there. I also catch larger fish in lakes and ponds.

Lakes and ponds are prime trout waters that should be accepted for what they are. They are different from streams and are a medium unto themselves. They are every bit as worthy of admiration, exultation, and rev-

erence because they are what they are, different. They produce some of the finest fly fishing for trout, bass, pike, panfish, etc., that can be found. We fly fishers sometimes try to project ourselves as saintly beings. We are not. We are human. We apply a certain amount of logic and intelligence to our sport. The lake fly fishing I have done has taught me some lessons about trout in impoundments. Trout can be spooky in still water as has been pointed out by several authors on the subject. Trout can also be mule stubborn. They can be oblivious to an approaching boat, a man's silhouette, or an anchor unceremoniously thrown overboard. At times, it seems there is no distraction that will deter them from gorging on subsurface midge pupae. I feel that nothing short of dynamite will deter these lake feeding trout from continuing to gorge themselves once they begin feeding. I have caught upwards of two dozen 13- to 17-inch trout, from a boat anchored in the same spot when trout are feeding heavily on midge pupae. The secret of this type of suc-cess is to be able to recognize what is happening on the surface and then translate that to what is happening near the bottom of the lake. All of the above-mentioned fish were hooked subsurface on a full-sinking line after a countdown technique was used to get the fly down to the feeding frenzy.

John Merwin goes on to point out that, "The astounding number of fly fishing books published since the 1930s have become the foundation of an angling technocracy that centers around streams." Lakes and ponds over the years have obviously not had an adequate press agent as have rivers and streams. I guess a movie titled *A Lake Runs Through It* just doesn't impart the same hint of romanticism as a title that suggests a river. It does not however depreciate the value of a lake to those who have learned to really love and appreciate them and their value to trout fishing.

In the following text I will present hints on a blue-collar approach to fly fishing and fly rod purchasing. I will provide helpful hints that have worked for me in the many facets of lake fly fishing. These tips include the use of a boat, float tube, clothing, swim fins, and other equipment to make the lake fly fisher more comfortable and more successful in pursuing the sport. I will list those flies that provided me with the many memories I carry into the writing of this book.

CHAPTER ONE

Equipment

Good equipment is essential to the enjoyment of any undertaking. Fly fishing is no exception. Good equipment does not have to mean new, very expensive equipment. Good equipment does mean getting the best your money can buy. Cost takes on a new meaning when it comes to personal safety. Reasonably priced new and used equipment can be purchased that allows for a high degree of safety and enjoyment when on the water.

BOATS

A boat is a floatable casting platform that is essential for lake fly fishing. Within reason, a boat cannot be too big. I have used 12-foot car-top boats and they work well on the small, high-country trout lakes. Car-toppers however, are generally not as stable as larger boats. I have an old 15 1/2-foot Smithcraft that has served me well for many years. It is very stable in rough water and allows plenty of room for gear and one companion when casting and retrieving. I have fished from this boat at a distance of seven miles off shore in the Sea of Cortez, with four people aboard. I also use it as a casting platform on small lakes such as Sunrise, Rainbow, Big Lake, and Concho in the White Mountains. I feel much at ease when the wind begins to blow. Anyone who has fished the high-country lakes in Arizona knows how rapidly the wind can come up and how hard it can blow. Even a small lake can quickly become a very-hard-to-navigate maelstrom.

Boats don't have to be purchased new. Persons on a limited budget, many times, can find a good buy on a boat of their choice in the want ads of their local newspaper. Often, a complete package of boat, motor, and trailer as well as additional accessories can be purchased for a fraction of their original new cost.

My Smithcraft was secured at no monetary cost to me in 1969. I made a deal where I received one boat free if I hauled two of them from Parker to Yuma, Arizona. The one I got unfortunately had a gaping two-foot hole in the bottom of it. But, for the cost of $53.00 I had the bottom heliarc welded. The weld has not failed to this day. The wooden decking has been replaced twice but the weld continues to hold.

Larger boats are generally more stable on the water than smaller craft.

Larger craft are not out of place on small lakes. They are easily pulled over the unimproved roads in the high country. If constructed of aluminum, they are also relatively easy to load and unload, even where the launching facilities may be somewhat rudimentary.

Car–toppers and canoes are very handy for getting into those lakes where a trailered boat just cannot be taken. Canoes tend to be very unstable when used as a platform in which to stand. Canoes make a decent platform on which to sit.

Aluminum boats should be tightly secured to their trailer when being towed over unimproved gravel roads. If a boat is allowed to bang around on the trailer, rivets loosen. The boat will begin to leak at the seams. Another cause of leaks in aluminum boats is by allowing heavy objects such as anchors, gas cans, etc. to bounce around inside the boat when it is towed over rough roads. This will also cause rivets to loosen and seams to leak.

Personal preference, technique, and safety will be some of the deciding factors on the selection of any boat.

MOTORS

Motors are of two types, gasoline and electric. Kirk would say there is one other type—oars. At 80 years of age he continued to row his boat when lake fly fishing. He had both gas and electric motors but sold them several years ago in favor of oars.

Again, motors may be purchased as part of a package thus cutting the costs drastically over their new counterparts.

In Arizona, most small trout lakes have some type of motor restriction. The current State or Indian Reservation Fishing Regulations should always be consulted regarding the status of a particular lake. A gasoline engine of 8 manufacturers–rated horsepower or an electric trolling motor will satisfy the requirements on most trout lakes in Arizona. A 10–horsepower engine will get a person off Sunrise Lake through moderately heavy wind. Motor restrictions do vary between the State and the White Mountain Apache Reservation.

An electric trolling motor is handy for those who prefer not to play with gasoline and prefer to troll flies or transport quietly. Some lakes are restricted to a single electric motor. A good, deep–cycle marine battery is a must to prolong running time.

FLOAT TUBES

Float tubes are another type of floatable casting platform essential to the lake fly fisher. Float tubes are also the primary life-support system to an angler on the water. These devices, in my opinion, should be purchased new, although surely they don't have to be. To me, they are a rather personal piece of fishing gear. Fly fishers who anticipate the purchase of a float tube should research those tubes available and buy the very best tube available. Fortunately there are several very good brands on the market today and improvements are constantly being made.

A quality tube should have at least two separate air chambers so that if one fails the other can support the person until shore is reached or help arrives. The tube should have a heavy yet durable nylon or other non-rotting synthetic cover with bright colors sewn in so that boaters on the lakes are made aware of the tuber's presence on the water. The purchase price of a very good tube can be amortized over the number of years of service received from that tube. Even though the purchase price may seem steep, the long-term average on a good tube is very reasonable. At this writing, I am beginning the tenth year of moderate use on my Buck's Bag. Except for some water stains, it shows little wear.

The air chambers (in my case, inner tubes) should be inspected periodically to be sure the seams are not about to fail. A punctured tube will normally lose its air rather slowly because of the low pressure involved. If an air chamber seam fails, the air can leave the chamber rapidly because the hole will resemble an extended knife slit. If the tube's cover is intact, it will slow the release of air and allow the tuber more time to reach safety. A good, serviceable life jacket should always be worn when tubing. A life jacket is the backup life-saving system if for some reason all air chambers fail simultaneously.

Some "U" tubes are constructed so that they keep the user in a constant butt down, feet up, slouched down position with the posture of fishing up hill. The end result of this impossible position is the shipping of water over the back of the waders. I saw a prime example of this at Stone Lake. My friend had borrowed a "U" tube specifically for this trip. The way the seat was constructed kept him slouched backward and when he left the water he always had to put on a complete change of dry clothing. He wondered why he had paid the price for a pair of neoprene waders if he was going to be sopping wet every time he fished from that tube. Fortunately I had an extra round tube along and my friend finished out the trip using it. The round tube allowed him to fish in an upright position and by doing so, did not allow water to over-top his chest waders. He purchased a round tube when he returned home.

It has been widely touted that the "U" tube is easier to get into and out of than the round tube. This may or may not be true. I have seen elderly people enter and exit "U" tubes with the near threat of great bodily injury. The fact that a tube may be easier or harder to get into and out of should not be the determining factor in the purchase of a tube. How the tube allows a person to fish when on the water should be the determining factor. Try to borrow and test-use the different types of tubes available prior to purchase. This will allow the individual a chance to determine first-hand, which tube best fits their needs and style.

Whether a tube should be round or "U" shaped is a matter of personal choice. Regardless of which is purchased it should be the most well constructed float tube you can afford.

The new kickboats are another option to explore. They incorporate some of the features of both boat and float tube. Their higher profile gives them a higher center of gravity and makes them somewhat more vulnerable to acting as a sail when the wind kicks up. Some models are usable on running waters. I have seen quite a number of them on the San Juan River in New Mexico. They normally range in price somewhere between a tube and a small boat.

WADERS

Waders should be the best a person can afford. Good waders can keep a person warm in 40-degree water temperatures. They can prolong the amount of time spent on the lake before the tuber must beach to warm up. They may prevent having to beach at all. Waders should be large enough to slip on and off comfortably. They should allow long johns, sweat pants, or other undergarments to be worn on the feet, legs, and butt. These garments aid greatly in buffering cold water temperatures. Should the tube fail, a person may find himself in the water longer then anticipated. The extra insulation of undergarments inside the waders may forestall hypothermia and allow for a safe return to shore.

While there are a good selection of waders available on the market today, the type needed for float tubing in trout waters can, in my opinion, be narrowed down rather quickly. Four to five millimeter, nylon covered, stocking-foot neoprene are my waders of choice. They are tough, don't crack, keep a person warm, and are generally available through the sporting goods mail-order houses at under $100.00. Additional undergarments can be worn quite comfortably under these waders. The waders will also aid in floating a person if the tube should fail. The waders, in tandem with a life preserver, should allow a person to get to shore, or at least stay afloat until help arrives. This is true in the unlikely event of a 100% tube bladder system failure.

An old pair of athletic socks can be worn over the foot part of the wader to prolong the life of the wader foot. The sock will take the punishment of walking in the waders on the shoreline and keep the nylon from wearing through. The socks will aid in prolonging the feet from leaking. Even better, but at a cost of about $20.00, is a neoprene booty which can be slipped over the wader foot offering greater resistance to wear.

A word of caution should be offered here regarding the use of these waders for stream fishing. A person should not plan to hike very far overland to get to their favorite fishing spot in these waders. They are very hot to walk in, especially during the warmer times of the year. I learned this lesson the hard way.

In spring 1988 I purchased a pair of brand-name 5-mm waders. In the fall of 1989 my friend Joe Clifford and I met his son Matt in Yellowstone Park where he was working as comptroller at the Lake Lodge on Yellowstone Lake. On September 13 we decided to hike in to the Upper Snake River near the south entrance of the Park. Twenty-two-year-old Matt assured us that it was only about a two-mile hike. Since we had to wade the Snake immediately after leaving the car it seemed natural to put the waders on before crossing. This being done we crossed the river and proceeded toward our destination. The two-mile hike turned into a nightmarish trek of about five miles. When I reached the Upper Snake I thought I was going to die. I pulled off the waders, inverted them to dump out the water (perspiration), and fished in my skivvies until the insides of this torture machine were dry. That afternoon, I draped those jewels around my neck and walked the five miles to the car in my underwear. The waders were donned to re-cross the river and immediately taken off again. Because of the heat generated inside the waders I subsequently lost the toenails off both my big toes. I don't do much hiking in my 5-mm waders anymore.

SWIM FINS

A good pair of swim fins designed to accommodate the float-tuber are essential. They are the propellers that push the tuber around the lake.

Swim fins for tubers are available in several styles and from most retail fly fishing and outdoor equipment mail-order houses. I was introduced to Force Fins several years ago by Dave Cohen of the Desert Fly Casters of Phoenix on a trip to Christmas Tree Lake on the Fort Apache Indian Reservation. This was after I had purchased a pair of Kickapoo Kickers. The Kickapoo Kickers operate on the principle that they will propel a person forward instead of backward. Most conventional swim fins propel the tuber backward in the water. I had very little success with the Kickers as I found them to be unmanageable whether the wind was blowing or not. They were especially troublesome in the wind because my legs were not strong enough to counter the action of the wind however gently it was blowing. I would sit in one spot and wear myself out pumping my legs and still never get anywhere.

Dave recognized my plight and let me borrow his Force Fins for a few hours. He almost didn't get them back. With them I had little difficulty navigating anywhere on the lake I chose to go, even under windy conditions. I ordered a pair when I returned from the trip. They continue to serve me well.

Care must be taken when putting the swim fins on so that they are securely fastened to the foot and that the fastening device will not work loose while navigating the lake. Fins have been irretrievably lost in deep silt. This can happen when the fins are not fastened securely or they were not tethered to the tuber's leg with an appropriate tethering system.

My system of applying swim fins is to: 1.) don my waders, 2.) put on a pair of neoprene booties, 3.) slip a foot into each fin, 4.) fasten the heel straps securely, 5.) secure the tethers to my ankles, and 6.) pull the gravel guards over the tethers so that they don't hang up on anything when I'm on the water. So far this system has served me well and I have yet to lose a fin.

Recently I have been using a product called Hurricane fins. These are very comfortable to wear and, in my opinion, allow the wearer to push as much water as the Force Fins. They cost about half the price of Force Fins, appear to be every bit as durable, and they float in open water.

Swim fins that float are very good if they come off only in open water. This does not solve the problem of burying them in deep silt. Whether the fins float or not they should be tethered securely to the tuber.

In very weedy conditions, a pair of ping pong paddles can free a tuber should the legs and fins become entangled in the submerged aquatic vegetation. Mid- to late-summer conditions can find many of the high-country lakes very weedy. The paddles can be modified to fit into one of the pockets of the tube.

FLY RODS

Fly rods are probably the most personal of all the gear a fly fisher owns. The spectrum ranges from priceless old Winstons that are locked in vaults, to modern-day split cane rods costing thousands of dollars. It includes graphite rods which cost hundreds of dollars and fiberglass rods which cost under $100.00.

After my trip to Sunrise Lake in October 1985, I explored rod costs and became somewhat discouraged at the apparent high cost of this basic element of the sport. I expanded my horizons however and sent requests in the mail to every retail outlet that I could find listed in a major fly fishing magazine. As the catalogs began to arrive I gained a new perspective on the purchase of a fly rod. I found an old friend, the Netcraft Company, where I had gotten fishing supplies when I was a boy in Illinois. There were also newly found friends such as The Hook and Hackle Company, who sold fly rod components. These components could produce a quality fly rod at less than half the price of a manufactured one. I ordered rod components from both of these companies and tested my ability to produce a rod with which I felt comfortable. The rods were produced and helped me attain some initial success in fly fishing. I still use those rods and have added several to my collection since then. Each rod, while inexpensive to purchase and fun to build, has been a pleasure to use and cumulatively have helped me land several thousand trout over the past 13 years.

For anyone who enjoys working with his or her hands, building a fly rod is very enjoyable, especially during the long winter months when fishing time may be limited or nonexistent.

I recently completed my dream rod for float-tube fishing. It is a 9-foot, 5-weight constructed on a Loomis GL3 blank. I use various 6-weight forward lines including a full-floating, a sink-tip, and both fast and intermediate full-sinking lines. My next project will be to build a 9-foot, 7-weight rod. The heavier rod will be for those times when the wind blows my 5-weight off the lake. That type of weather occurs rather frequently at 9000-plus feet elevation in Arizona.

To date I have used 5-, 6-, 7- and 8-weight rods to a maximum length of 9 1/2 feet. These rods have served well and will also continue to be used as needed.

Eight-weight rods with a bass bug taper line are the rule when casting large bass bugs in windy conditions on lakes such as Rainbow, Woodland, Concho, Show Low, Fools Hollow, and Scott's Reservoir.

FLY REELS

It is difficult to build your own fly reel. One is pretty well resigned to purchasing something already made. Fly reels come in a broad spectrum of sizes and prices.

A fly reel should be sized to the rod used and the type of fishing to be done. Kirk once told me a person should buy the cheapest reel that could be found. All it did was hold the fly line when it wasn't being used. I have learned much since I was given that advice.

Inexpensive reels that function well are unbelievably better than cheap reels that don't function at all. I purchased two Berkley graphite reels with press-on spools for under $20.00 each in 1986. Extra spools were available at that time for under $10.00. They were the middleweight models of the three models then available. I still receive some incredulous looks when I show up with my inexpensive reels with the various spools that press on the reel frame, shimmed with a rubber band. This model has since been replaced with one that has a positive lock-and-release button on the spool. The two reels I purchased back in 1986 are still serving me well and I have landed over a thousand fish, mostly trout, with my inexpensive reels. I have taken trout of up to five pounds on them and they continue to function well. Periodic maintenance (as is needed on any reel) has kept them operational and able to function under the pressures of landing a five-pound rainbow in heavy water.

The reel should be capable of holding the weight line of choice and 50 to 100 yards of 18- to 20-pound Dacron backing. The backing serves a dual purpose. It is available for those long runs that a very large trout might make when it is hooked. It also serves to widen the coils of the fly line. This tends to somewhat flatten out the kinks if the line has been stored on the reel for any length of time.

FLY LINES

Fly lines are matched to both the rod and the reel on which they are used. Fly rods are normally labeled near the butt just above the grip as to the weight of line for which they were designed.

Commercial vinyl cleaner is very good for cleaning and prolonging the life of modern fly lines. This cleaner will float a sinking line the first few times after application. Several long casts and a few trout later, however, and voilá the line sinks again.

Most line manufacturers, as well as rod designers, allow that when using a weight–forward line a person can use a line one weight heavier than that designated for the rod (i.e., 5–weight rod and 6–weight forward line). Weight–forward lines do not use as much space on a reel spool as double taper or level lines.

LEADERS

I was pleased to read Paul Schullery's article in the May–June 1991 issue of *American Angler* regarding the myth about leaders. Paul is the author of *Mountain Time* and *American Fly Fishing: A History*. In essence, Paul felt great relief when he found out that fish don't read the books on leader construction, length, or size. He became aware that what works for him is what he uses in a given situation. After having read his article, I felt great relief to know that my unorthodox method of leadering my fly line may have suddenly become acceptable to someone other than myself. What I do works and the proof that the fish don't know the difference is in the success I continue to have using this "system."

First I clip the end of my fly line to a square end. Then I pound a no–knot eyelet into the end of the line. To this metal eyelet I secure a length of two– to six–pound–test Magna Thin or one of the other new, small diameter, co–polymer monofilament fishing lines now available. The length I usually choose is about equal to the length of fly rod. The fly is then secured to the end of the monofilament and I am ready to start fishing. I fish this leader until it is trimmed back to about the length of my arm. Then I tie on a new piece and start over. It is a simple "formula" and has proven to work for me on both streams and lakes and in both dry fly and subsurface applications. I have had extremely good success on the San Juan River in New Mexico fishing both wet and dry. I caught and released 49 grayling on May 5, 1989 dry–fly fishing a size 14 Coachman Trude on Lee Valley Lake in the White Mountains using this leader formula. This is the only leader formula that I use 99 percent of the time.

I do have one or two tapered leaders that I use at times when fishing with Joe Clifford. He has trouble understanding my crude methods sometimes. The tool called the "Tie Fast Knot Tyer" makes it easy and very enjoyable to tie nail knots when joining backing to the fly line or a leader to the fly line (when one uses a tapered or knotted leader).

I didn't invent the "system" I use. I have my old friend Kirk to thank for introducing it to me. I wish I were smart enough to have thought of it. Thanks again to Paul Schullery for making me feel more at ease with what I now consider a very orthodox leader formula.

FLIES

The wet flies I use for lake fishing are generally unweighted (see more on this in Chapter Two). In order for these flies to take on the appearance of a live insect, crustacean, minnow, or other type of pond/lake life form, I try to add materials to my flies that allow them greater lifelike movement in still water. I don't feel that glitter is as important as the ability of the fly to pulsate and show great movement. One of the materials that adds great movement to any wet fly is marabou. The Yeager Damsel is a good example with its short marabou tail along with the marabou side wings. I am in the process of experimenting with such patterns as the Montana Nymph, Gold Ribbed Hare's Ear Nymph, and the Peacock Lady series by adding marabou to the tails in place of the stiff hackle fiber tails called for in their original pattern formulas.

Reversing the hackles on a Woolly Bugger (tie in by the butt) so that the barbs flare forward, I feel, imparts greater movement to the fly. Hackles should be the webbiest possible.

CHAPTER TWO

Techniques

Good technique is necessary for good equipment to work to its full potential. Nontraditional techniques can be good if they produce the desired results. In this chapter, I will describe those techniques that have worked for me over the past 12 years.

BOATS

As noted in Chapter One, boats are effective casting platforms for lake fly fishers.

Boats have many different configurations. For purposes of this text, the primary configuration I refer to will be the small 12- to 16-foot V–hull fishing boat. Application of the following techniques to other hull configurations may need modification by the user for both practicality and safety.

Wind plays a very important part in using a boat to its best advantage when on a lake. Before getting into various methods of dealing with the wind, I would like to explain what the wind does to a lake.

Windy conditions prevail on Arizona's high–country lakes at least a little, almost every day of the year. Usually it will blow steadily from a single direction (i.e., from the southwest ahead of a winter cold front). When this occurs, a current is set up in the lake similar to the current in a stream. The harder the wind blows, the stronger the current. Water actually stacks up on the far end of the lake towards which the wind is blowing. When the water is pushed to the far shore it reverses its flow under the lake surface and returns below the surface in the direction from which the wind is blowing. This current causes mixing of the lake and can tend to break down stratification in the water column. It can be difficult to get a fly to sink to an appropriate depth when strong currents prevail in a lake.

Positioning a boat in calm conditions requires little more than finding the right spot to fish and dropping anchor. A more quiet approach can be made by drifting slowly into the spot without dropping anchor. I have used both methods and prefer using an anchor. This allows the angler to remain in the same general area when the inevitable wind begins to blow.

Stalking individual fish can be done in calm weather with the use of oars or an electric trolling motor. It has been my experience that being able to stalk individual feeding trout is by far the exception rather than the rule when lake fly fishing. The opportunities just don't seem to present themselves to me that often.

Most trips are spent looking for underwater structure such as weed beds. Insect hatches on the surface that may have relevance to what is happening many feet below are also sought. Different forms of trout food must be recognized to broaden the anglers consideration of which fly will match the local hatch.

Previous successes and familiarity with a particular lake also helps the fly fisher to return to that secret honey hole and select the "right" fly.

Usually, when fishing over structure or a midge hatch, one anchor amidships functions well. The anchor should be positioned on the opposite side of the boat from where you're fishing. This serves two purposes. First, it keeps the anchor rope away from any fish that may be hooked. Secondly, the anchor will set better on the lake bottom if the anchor rope is allowed to be fully extended on the off side. I keep the anchor rope and the wind at my back as much as possible.

When the wind begins to blow in earnest, I usually remove the anchor amidships and anchor directly off the bow of the boat. When it blows that hard I also use a second anchor which is tied to the transom. This anchor is put on a fairly short rope. This keeps the stern of the boat from swing-ing back and forth like a pendulum. The pendulum action, along with the lake current, usually will not allow a fly to sink to the proper depth. Tim Rogers describes a method using three anchors in an article in the June 1995 issue of *Flyfishing* magazine. This technique calls for anchors at the stern on both port and starboard sides as well as an anchor at the bow.

I have found that even under windy conditions, if the fly is kept down in the area where the trout are actively feeding they can continue to be caught. I caught and released 22 rainbows between 13 and 16 inches at one of my favorite lakes on April 27th, 1988. These trout were caught on a size 16 Yellow Midge Pupa. This action occurred while I was anchored in a single spot with the wind gusting to 25 miles per hour.

Drift fishing can be effective. In breezy conditions this technique works reasonably well. In windy conditions however, it can be difficult to keep the fly at the proper depth. The wind will normally push the boat along broadside. This accelerates the rate at which the fly is elevated toward the lake surface. Dragging a small anchor can help slow the sail effect of the boat, thus allowing the fly to sink. Another name for this technique might be wind trolling.

Trolling flies is another method that can be effective. A motor of some sort is usually used to propel the boat. It also allows great maneuverability even in windy conditions. Oars are also a means of propulsion for trolling.

Grace and I went fishing on April 11, 1992. While I rowed the boat, she trolled a size 12 Shiner off the transom. She caught and released 24 rainbows that day. This was the most fish of any kind she had ever caught.

My personal preference when fishing from a boat is to anchor in one spot and cast to structure, an insect hatch, or some other lake feature that looks productive.

MOTORS

Gasoline engines have about the same uses as electric trolling motors, but they are generally more powerful. They can be used for trolling as well as general transport. They are usually better for transporting in windy conditions and provide a longer running time.

The use of a motor, be it gas, electric or man power (oars) is a personal preference that can cost from under $50.00 to over $1000.00. Motors may be used by fly fishers to transport themselves to their chosen spot on a lake. They may be used to maneuver in the wind. They may be used for trolling. They are invariably used to return to the launching ramp safely.

I use a trolling motor to transport myself around a lake. Often I will troll a fly from where I was fishing, to my new destination. I catch fish trolling. I have never caught the sheer numbers of trout while trolling that I have when anchored and casting to preferred structure in a lake. I can say the same for the sizes of the trout caught. My personal best, casting with a fly rod from a boat, is an 18.5–inch rainbow trout taken from Sunrise Lake on September 18, 1987. My largest trout trolling has not exceeded 16 inches. This is probably not a fair comparison however, as I don't troll in the same proportion timewise as I spend casting and stripping.

There was a day on Sunrise Lake (June 12, 1987) when the only trout I could catch was taken by trolling a size 10 Gold Hair–winged Streamer. A friend and I fished from 8:30 in the morning until 2:30 in the afternoon. I managed one small rainbow and two small brook trout on the day I fished with flies. My friend fished with spinning gear and small spinners. He got skunked. He is unnamed here because to embarrass him twice would cost me a friend.

State and Indian Reservation regulations should be reviewed to determine the motor allowable on any of the high–country lakes. Beyond that consideration, the angler must decide which type will get a person(s) on and off the water the safest and most efficiently.

FLOAT TUBES

In 1989 I found a Buck's Bag under the Christmas tree. At that time I had no idea how much fun "surfing" for trout could be. I have since logged some 1200+ hours in "the tube." I have read several books and articles regarding the use of float tubes. There is a lot of good information on their use already in print. Authors such as Dave Whitlock, Deke Meyer, and Del

Canty should be read and their directions followed. I offer a few thoughts of my own in the following paragraphs.

I find myself in constant motion when tubing. On most days there is some wind. Even when a lake is calm, I find myself constantly on the move. When it is calm I have to make a conscious effort to stop kicking if I want to stay in one spot. It feels unnatural for me not to be finning with the swim fins.

Propulsion in the tube is backward so it sometimes seems that the action is one of constant trolling. Normally, when battling the wind, the effort is to keep from letting the wind carry me to the other side of the lake. I like to keep on the move so I am not facing into the wind. It's easy to drag a fly behind the tube when facing into the wind but casting into that same wind can be very difficult.

It can be difficult to keep a fly at the proper depth in windy conditions when tubing. Since I don't normally weight my flies, this becomes more acute (more on this later in the chapter).

The technique that I prefer when tubing is to remain ever so slightly on the move. This is especially true early in the year before weed beds have gotten established. Similarly, as with fishing from a boat, I cast my fly for as much distance as I can, count down to the appropriate depth and use a very slow retrieve. Early in the year, slow seems to always be better than fast in my opinion. As the weather warms and water temperatures approach 60 degrees, many times a very rapid retrieve is more effective. I learned this quite by accident on September 6, 1994. I was fishing one of my favorite high-country lakes on that day. It was rather blustery and rainy for a late summer day. When I started at 9:20 a.m., the air temperature was 73 degrees and the water surface was 62 degrees. There was a heavy filamentous algae bloom in the lake as is usual there in late summer. I was having moderate success with the patterns I was using with a catch rate of three fish per hour for the first two hours. In between squalls, I would sit in my camper waiting for the lightning to subside. During one of these waits, an older model pickup truck pulled into the parking lot and stopped. A single fisherman got out, rigged a fly rod, launched an inner tube with a strap on it, and began to fish. At first I didn't pay much attention to this guy who liked to play Russian roulette with Thor. One of the camper windows was open however, and after a while I was aware that I was continuing to hear fish splashing on the surface of the water. I started to pay attention to what this man was doing. He was sitting in his inner tube just off shore and casting out over a large weed bed just beyond him. No sooner did his line hit the water than he would begin an all-out effort to swim his fly back to himself as rapidly as he possibly could. He seldom got the fly back without a brook trout taking the fly and going along for the ride. He selectively culled out six of the largest brookies and left the water. He was there less than an hour. Before I could corner him to ask him about his method and what pattern he was using, he was gone. I wondered if he was using some pattern that was super productive or if his success was attributable only to the rapid retrieve. When the next break in the storm came I was back on the water as quickly as I could get there. I swapped my full uniform sink line for a sink–tip and began to experiment with the very rapid retrieve. It worked so well that I increased my catch rate by 1.5 fish per hour over the next four hours. Takes which produced no fish outnumbered those landed by more than two to one. I also experimented with patterns. It was interesting in that it didn't seem to make any difference what pattern I used. The takes would come with the rapid retrieve and would cease when I slowed it down to my normal early season slow method. I have since used this rapid retrieve on most other lakes during the warmer part of the year and have found it to be quite productive.

Float tubes should be kept properly inflated. A fully inflated tube will float higher on the water. The higher profile can make distance casting easier. When fully inflated, the tube will be much easier to propel through the water. Leg cramps are less likely to occur. It is hardly tiring to fin along for several hours at a time when the tube is fully inflated. I find that the more relaxed I remain in the tube the longer I can remain in the water. When I tighten up and try to out–kick the force of the wind, invariably I cramp up and must leave the water. Conversely, I have found I can move against the wind in a slower more relaxed mode and prolong the amount of time I spend on the water. A float tube is not designed for speed. I try to never get in a hurry, even when my bladder is crying for relief. Slow here is also better than fast. I have yet to try the electric motors for tubes now on the market. Maybe when I'm 90.

WEIGHT (LINES AND FLIES)

An angler can read reams of material on the pros and cons of using sinking lines, floating lines, sink–tip lines, as well as weighted versus unweighted flies. Again, the principle I apply here is, whatever works for the individual is appropriate for the occasion.

Kirk introduced me to the full–sinking line on my trip to Sunrise Lake in October 1985. It worked then and it continues to work for me. I have however, expanded on the original form of that idea. I now carry a medium sinking line for rather calm days. On those days when the wind wants to challenge my presence on the lake, I use a fast–sinking line to cut through the current. For relatively shallow lakes, I use a sink–tip line to swim my fly over the shallow bottom or the tops of thick growing weed beds. On the seemingly rare occasions when dry–fly fishing presents itself, I use a full floating line. Other authors have also suggested having this variety of lines to meet whatever challenge may arise.

If I were to purchase only one line, however, it would be a medium full-sinking line.

As has been described in many other publications on the subject, some 90 percent of the food taken by trout is consumed below the water's surface. That is the area of the water column where I concentrate 98 percent of my efforts.

There are also pros and cons for the values of using weighted or unweighted flies. When I first started tying flies I religiously followed the pattern formulas. When it called for weighting the fly with lead fuse wire, like the lemmings I followed the piper's directions. Sometime from then to now, I quit tying lead fuse wire weighted flies for use in lakes. I let the sinking line do the work of getting the fly to the proper depth. The old master, E.H. "Polly" Rosborough, never added weight to his nymphs, even for stream fishing (*Fly Tyer*, Spring 1985). He felt that weight in flies destroys their center of gravity and imparts something less than a natural action to the fly. I have adopted his philosophy for the most part. Unweighted flies have certainly worked very well for me.

One exception to the unweighted fly philosophy is the recent use of beads at the fly-tying bench. Beads of various forms, made of such materials as brass, nickel, glass, and plastic have become commonplace in the tying of many fly patterns. Bead-bodied flies are not only attractive but they catch fish. Flies tied with metal bead heads provide some weight that helps to sink the fly, while allowing it to act like a living insect in still water. This provides some relief when fishing in windy conditions. The metal head helps the fly to sink but still allows the materials on the body to continue to pulsate like the living creature it is trying to simulate. Plastic beads provide the bead-bodied effect while adding virtually no weight to the fly. Unfortunately the plastic beads usually have a thin coating of color over the bead base. After just a few hard takes by hungry trout, the color is gone and replaced by the white plastic base. I have found however, that hungry trout will still take the fly with just the whites of the eyes showing.

Weighting wet flies for stream fishing probably makes more sense to me than weighting lake flies. Bud Lilly was a great advocate of weighted flies for stream fishing. In his *Guide To Western Fly Fishing* he states, "What my guides and I often did, and what many of my friends do, is carry a spool of lead wire or fuse wire, and take a few turns around the body of the fly with it." Those little critters wash down in the current and a trout has little time to make its decision on whether or not to take the lure. Most times the nymph is taken because of a flash of color or a familiar shape imprinted in the trout through previous feeding habits.

Swimming a nymph or other type of wet fly in a lake requires more natural movement. This is because a fish has the opportunity to leisurely inspect the lure before it is taken.

I have extremely good success with the system I now use. Even in very windy weather I still catch good numbers of trout. When it gets so windy that I can't sink the fly properly, I go home. By then it's probably not safe to be on the water anyway.

My technique for fishing a subsurface fly goes something like this: I locate the spot that I want to fish, I cast for distance to the structure or hatch or area that I have located. I count down to various depths until the fly is taken either on the fall or on the strip. I then concentrate on that depth with subsequent retrieves.

My slow retrieve is very simple. First, I always keep my rod tip pointed directly at the fly. This includes keeping the rod tip constantly submerged in an effort to keep a tight (straight) line between the rod grip and the fly. The retrieve consists of one to three very sharp strips from four to eight inches in length. These are followed by a pause to let the fly fall. I continue this stripping method until I have retrieved all of the line or until a trout takes the fly. When the take comes, I lift the rod tip and the trout virtually hooks itself. It normally takes several minutes to retrieve the 40 to 60 feet of line I cast. If there is no take, I repeat the process. A few takes come during the countdown as the fly, like me, is constantly in motion. The greatest number of takes by far however, come while the fly is being stripped back to the tube.

As mentioned previously in this chapter, I use this slow retrieve when water temperatures are below 55 degrees early in the year. It's a simple method that fits my style very well. I have read of some really complicated stripping techniques, but I find that when I get on the water I have a devil of a time remembering the cadences or sequences of all the different retrieves. The method I use works for me so I don't concern myself with all the others. My retrieves are simple, be they slow or fast, and have been very effective. Five species of trout, largemouth bass, bluegill and green sunfish, and golden shiners have all succumbed to this seductive technique.

This method has been effective whether fishing from a boat, a float tube, or wading the shoreline.

I use a fast retrieve when a slow one doesn't work. Often times the speed of the retrieve is dictated by warmer water temperatures. A high percentage of the time my slow retrieve is rewarded with numerous takes.

I have read that flies should be retrieved in a certain direction when fish-ing a lake. The most prominent example I can think of is that damselfly nymphs should be retrieved from deep to shallow water. That is toward the shore. I have however, found damselfly nymphs in deep water swimming in all directions. Many times they are swimming to the east shore when the west shore is closer. I have also found that when fishing a damselfly nymph, I have had great success in fishing it in about any direction I care to. The basic premise to this success is that the trout are actively feeding on these nymphs. I have fished the very center of small lakes equidistant to any shore, fished in all directions and caught trout in all directions. Again, an angler should experiment with methods and do whatever works.

Neither the trout nor the insect populations read these books. To me these reference books are points of departure but should not be the total substance of a person's individual effort. Continued experimentation should always be the order of the day.

The author on Rainbow Lake.

CHAPTER THREE

Etiquette and Safety

I had planned to go into a rather protracted essay on etiquette. The more I thought about it however, the more I realized that the whole subject could be summed up as follows: Do unto others as you would have them do unto you.

SAFETY

Most authorities on float tubing discourage the practice of tubing alone. I certainly don't disagree with this advice. I do, however, also accept the philosophy of Robert Alley in his book *Advanced Lake Fly Fishing: The Skillful Tuber* he states "If I followed the rule of never tubing alone, I'd seldom fish."

I retired in August of 1991 with the intent of doing as much fishing as I possibly could. Most of my friends were working and continue to do so. If I didn't fish alone I would be defeating the purpose for which I retired.

For those of us who insist on the loner approach, there are a number of safety points that should be addressed:

1. Always let someone know where you are going and how long you intend to be there.

2. Keep physically fit. Use your exercise machine regularly, walk, jog, etc., to keep your cardiovascular system in a state of readiness to perform the rigors of tubing a 9000–foot–elevation lake for several hours; you'll be glad you did when the wind comes up. You also may have to walk out carrying all your gear.

3. Keep your vehicle, boat, tube, motor, and other primary modes of transportation in good operating condition. Breakdowns in remote country are not only costly in both time and money, they can also be life threatening.

4. State and Reservation boating regulations require the carrying of Coast Guard approved personal floatation devices for each person riding in a watercraft within that jurisdiction. Common sense

dictates that this carry over to float tubing. I always wear a life jacket when tubing, whether I am alone or with someone. Even during the summer, the life jacket is my backup system and a hedge against disaster if all else fails.

5. When tubing, don't do anything in a hurry. This applies to getting into and out of a tube, finning around a lake, or getting into or out of the water. Float tubing is not a speed sport.

6. A wading staff or long stout stick can help tubers keep their balance when getting into or out of a float tube.

7. Float tubes should be used in still waters, but not in running waters.

8. Dress warmly under the waders including the feet. Silk and/or polypropylene are very lightweight yet warm. Hypothermia is always a concern in cold water, high-country lakes.

9. A silk or wool scarf, turtleneck tee shirt, or sweater can do much to keep body heat from escaping at the neck.

10. A good hat will keep the sun from cooking the brain in the summer and allow for the retention of body heat in cold weather.

11. A sunblock of at least SPF 15 is advisable at high altitude where sunlight is less filtered than at lower elevations. Sunblock is also highly recommended on cloudy days.

12. Even though it can be a real chore to climb out on the shoreline to relieve oneself, tubers should carry a supply of water to maintain body fluids. This is especially true if one plans to spend four or more continuous hours on the water. Dehydration can be a problem even when surrounded by a lake full of water.

CHAPTER FOUR

Southwestern Lake (& Stream) Flies

The flies listed in this chapter are by no means the only good lake flies. More information on other effective lake fly patterns can be found through the references given in the Bibliography. There are other local patterns that

The author tied all flies illustrated in this chapter.

are successful but not advertised. The flies that follow are those patterns that have become most familiar to me.

The patterns listed are those that have been used successfully either by the author or other local fly fishers. I'm sure that when this list is published, there will be those who feel slighted that their favorite fly was not included. This list is intended to be a point of departure, it will need revision and will never be complete. I'm hopeful some standardization of nomenclature will result from this effort.

When tying the patterns listed in this work, most flies were hackled rather sparsely when compared to other similar patterns sold in local sporting goods stores. Bodies are tied with fine and extra fine chenille or otherwise made on the lean side. I have had great success with the sparsely hackled flies tied in the smaller sizes. Most of the patterns I use are tied on various length size 12 and smaller hooks. Sizes 8 and 10 are also used. I tie most patterns in larger sizes for those anglers who prefer to have them on a larger hook.

The short-tailed Buggers illustrated in the pages that follow, while similar to the "Short Buggers" described by Steve Probasco in an article of the same name presented in *American Angler & Fly Tyer*, Winter 1988, were developed as "short-tailed" Buggers. In my original ties I had problems with fish hitting short when fishing them. I began to pinch the tails shorter and shorter until the take was at the hook. Now when I tie these flies I pinch (not cut) the tail off at approximately the same length as the length of the fly body. I often pinch the tail down as needed while fishing. Sometimes I end up with a tail that is no more than a tuft but the takes are at the hook, which has greatly increased my success. I began experimenting with the shortened tail during the summer of 1986 with the Yeagerburger and the Tom Knight patterns. I now tie the majority of the Buggers for my personal use in this manner. The hackle on those Buggers is always tied in by the butt and rather sparsely palmered forward.

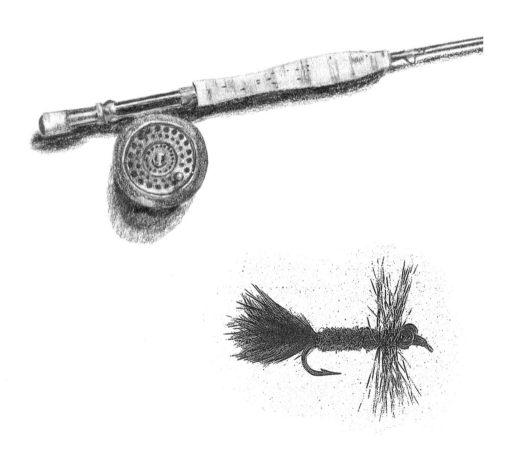

Yeagerburger (wet)

This fly is the result of experimenting with an old standby, the Woolly Bugger. In spring 1993 this pattern replaced the Sparrow (gray) as the number one fly in my lake fly arsenal. There are several patterns in this series: the dark, medium, and light olive Buggers and the Newcommer. All work well in our small lakes where there are good populations of snails, damselfly and dragonfly nymphs. The dark pattern has been the most productive to date.

      Hook: Mustad 9672, 3X.
 Hook Size: 8 to 14.
    Thread: Dark olive 6/0.
       Tail: Black marabou (short), pinched off (not cut), about the length of the body.
      Body: Medium, fine, X–fine dark olive chenille.
   Hackle: Grizzly saddle, full body palmer, tied in by the butt.
     Head: Tying thread.
   Source: The author, 1988.

Black Teaser (wet)

This pattern has been so productive I felt that it deserved a name. Basically, it is a black Woolly Worm with sparsely palmered brown hackle tied in by the butt. For my own use, I tie this on a size 12 or 14 down-eye 2X hook. It is suggestive of the midge pupae that hatch by the millions in most of the high–country lakes. A pattern of this description was written about as early as 1657 by Thomas Barker (Alley, 1991). While grouped in the general category of Woolly Worm, this pattern, with its proven ability to take trout consistently, qualifies it for a name of its own.

      Hook: Mustad 9671, 2X.
 Hook Size: 12 to 14.
    Thread: Black 6/0.
      Body: X–fine black chenille.
   Hackle: Brown saddle, full body palmer, tied in by the butt.
     Head: Tying thread.
   Source: Robert Alley, 1991.

Sparrow, Gray (wet)

This fly was discovered in the Summer 1986 edition of *Fly Tyer*, now *American Angler*, in an article written by Bob Harris. Jack Gartside, publisher and former teacher from Massachusetts, originated the fly. It was the number-one lake fly in my arsenal until just recently. It is effective in natural gray, olive, and brown. It is a producer in all the White Mountain lakes in which it is used. The largest trout taken with this pattern to date has been a 22-inch Apache (Arizona native trout) at Christmas Tree Lake on May 6, 1990. It was taken on a size 12 gray pattern.

Hook:	Mustad 9672, 3X.
Hook Size:	12 to 14.
Thread:	Black or gray 6/0.
Tail:	Gray pheasant flank feather (marabou type) or gray marabou pinched off short.
Body:	The tail feather wrapped forward on the hook shank or dubbed natural dark hare's ear Hare-Tron.
Hackle:	Pheasant rump feather, natural blue/green.
Collar:	Gray filoplume.
Head:	Tying thread.
Source:	Bob Harris, 1986.

Peacock Lady (wet)

The Peacock Lady is one of the most widely used flies in the White Mountains. Everybody has heard of this peacock-bodied fly. There are a number of versions of this popular fly. The basic formula I give here is patterned after the one Gordon Mankins described in *Patterns of the Masters* (1991). Local variations of this pattern include a red hackle fiber tail, no rib, various colored fore and aft hackles, and on and on. The version I used has the red hackle fiber tail. However it is tied, it remains a very popular fly.

Hook:	Mustad 79580, 4X.
Hook Size:	8 to 14.
Thread:	Black 6/0.

Tail: Golden pheasant tippets, red hackle fibers, or red marabou pinched off short.
Rear Hackle: Grizzly, saddle.
Body: Peacock herl, wrapped with tying thread.
Rib: Fine oval, gold or silver tinsel.
Front Hackle: Coachman brown, saddle.
Head: Tying thread.
Source: Gordon Mankins, 1991.

Becker Lake Special (wet)

This is one of those flies I heard about before I ever saw it. It seemed rather mysterious until finally viewed. It is very simple to tie and is effective in most of the area lakes including Becker and Horseshoe Cienega lakes.

Hook: Mustad 9672, 3X.
Hook Size: 8 to 14.
Thread: Brown 6/0.
Tail: Red acrylic yarn tied in a loop.
Body: Medium, fine, X–fine brown chenille.
Hackle: Brown saddle, full body palmer, tied in by the butt.
Head: Tying thread.
Source: Unknown

Gold Ribbed Hare's Ear Nymph (wet)

This is an all-time favorite wherever mayfly nymphs are fished. It is also effective in lakes where midge hatches occur. All of the White Mountain lakes qualify for this old favorite. It is especially effective at Lee Valley and Becker lakes.

Hook: Mustad 3906, Std.
Hook Size: 10 to 18.
Thread: Tan 6/0.
Tail: Mallard flank or hare's mask guard hairs.
Body: Dubbed natural hare's ear fur.
Wing Case: Turkey tail.
Rib: Fine gold wire or fine oval tinsel.
Legs or Beard: Picked–out dubbing or brown or badger hackle fibers.
Head: Tying thread.
Source: Jack Dennis, 1974.

Sparrow, Light Olive (wet)

This pattern has been very successful at Christmas Tree Lake on the Fort Apache Indian Reservation. On May 28, 1995 four of us took over 100 trout with this fly, most of which were native Apache trout. The native trout ranged from 15 to 19 inches. Brown trout caught were generally smaller. Even when the filoplume collar was chewed off, the fly continued to be effective. We probably went through at least a dozen of these before the day was over. All the flies were size 12. The Olive Sparrow also took a 19-inch brown trout at Reservation Lake on July 24, 1995. It also produced well at Pacheta Lake on July 28, 1994. All of the aforementioned lakes are on the Fort Apache Indian Reservation. All of the trout were released back into the lake.

Hook:	Mustad 9672, 3X.
Hook Size:	8 to 14.
Thread:	Olive 6/0.
Tail:	Pheasant flank feather dyed olive (marabou type) or light olive marabou pinched off short.
Body:	The tail feather wrapped forward on the hook shank or dubbed olive Hare-Tron.
Hackle:	Pheasant rump feather, natural blue/green, dyed olive or golden yellow.
Collar:	Olive-dyed filoplume.
Head:	Tying thread.
Source:	Bob Harris, 1986.

Shiner (wet)

Most fly tiers do at least some experimenting with new patterns. I am no exception. The Eyeflies were the end result of that experimentation during the winter of 1992. This black-bodied (black eye = shiner) fly has been the most productive of the Eyefly series to date. It is also tied in peacock, olive, gray, brown, and black with pearlescent rib. A drop of super glue between the eyes makes this a very durable fly. This fly has been very productive on both Concho and Mexican Hay lakes when Mexican Hay

Lake was a viable fishery. Unfortunately, Mexican Hay Lake has become a victim of water rights use. The water rights are held for irrigation of crops downstream and the Irrigation District has chosen to no longer store water sufficient to support a trout population. This lake no longer produces the large trout of years past.

Hook:	Mustad 79580, 4X.
Hook Size:	12 to 14.
Thread:	Black 6/0.
Tail:	Black marabou (short), pinched off (not cut), 1/2 to 3/4 the length of the body.
Body:	X–fine black chenille.
Hackle:	Grizzly saddle, palmer the front 1/3 of the body, tied in by the butt.
Head:	Tying thread.
Eyes:	Black, 2mm.
Source:	The author, 1992.

Yellow Midge Pupa (wet)

This is a pattern taken from *Popular Fly Patterns* by Terry Hellekson and attributed to Al Troth. As noted in Chapter Two, this pattern can be dynamite when trout are feeding on midge pupae near the lake bottom. This pattern is fished deep and slow with a natural ascent to the surface. Many times the  take comes while the fly is rather deep. I have, however, had it taken just before lifting it from the water for the next cast. It pays to continue the slow steady retrieve to the surface. It can be used successfully on all the lakes since they all contain large midge populations.

Hook:	Mustad 9671, 2X.
Hook Size:	12 to 16.
Thread:	Brown 6/0.
Tail/Butt:	Gray ostrich herl.
Body:	Yellow floss.
Rib:	Peacock herl and fine gold wire.
Legs:	Brown hackle fibers.
Collar:	Brown saddle hackle, tied back wet style.
Head:	Dubbed hare's ear fur.
Source:	Terry Hellekson, 1984.

Gray Teaser (wet)

This is another very simple pattern that I have given a name because of its special standing on lakes such as Horseshoe Cienega, Becker, and Sunrise. It is a slate gray Woolly Worm with either black or blue dun hackle. It is also suggestive of the many midge pupae found in the White Mountain lakes. It is highly effective when retrieved very slowly through the channels in weed beds. An 18.5–inch rainbow responded to such coaxing on Sunrise Lake in September 1987. This is a very easily tied pattern. A wise old fly tier once stated that some of the most effective nymph patterns are nondescript gray, have neither top nor bottom, and are simple to tie. This fly fits all those criteria.

   Hook: Mustad 9671, 2X.
 Hook Size: 10 to 16.
  Thread: Black 6/0.
   Body: X–fine charcoal gray chenille.
  Hackle: Black or blue dun saddle, full body palmered, tied in by
      the butt.
   Head: Tying thread.
  Source: The author, 1986.

Peacock's Eye (wet)

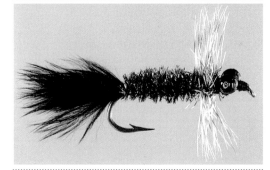

This is another pattern in the Eyefly series and is another good producer. Like its brother the Shiner, it is the result of experimentation. I have had good success with this fly on dark, windy, overcast days when nothing else seems to work.

   Hook: Mustad 79580, 4X.
 Hook Size: 12 to 14.
  Thread: Black 6/0.
   Tail: Black marabou (short), pinched off (not cut), about 1/3 to 1/2
      the length of the body.
   Body: Peacock herl, wrapped with tying thread.
  Hackle: Grizzly saddle, palmer the front 1/3 of body, tied in by the butt.
   Head: Tying thread.
   Eyes: Black, 2mm.
  Source: The author, 1992.

Coachman Trude (dry)

This is another pattern that was borrowed from Terry Hellekson's fine book *Popular Fly Patterns*. Some of the best dry–fly fishing I have ever experienced was with the Coachman Trude. That occurred at Lee Valley Lake in 1989. Grayling had been introduced into the lake the previous year. These fish were in the 12- to 14-inch range and absolutely loved this fly. The grayling have not fared well through the severe winters at 9400 feet in elevation. The year following this great fishing, the lake suffered a complete winterkill. Success at reestablishing the grayling since then has met with mixed results.

Hook:	Mustad 7957B, 1X.
Hook Size:	12 to 16.
Thread:	Black 6/0.
Tail:	Golden pheasant tippet.
Body:	Peacock herl.
Rib:	Fine gold wire.
Wing:	White calf tail.
Hackle:	Coachman (dark) brown, dry–fly quality.
Head:	Tying thread.
Source:	Terry Hellekson, 1984.

Lee Valley Lake.

Warden's Worry (wet)

I was first introduced to this pattern through John McKim's fine book *Fly Tying: Adventures in Fur, Feathers and Fun.* As a novice fly tier, this was one of the first patterns I learned to tie. According to John, it originated with the late A. L. Crupp of Chama, New Mexico. Mr. Crupp tied it with an aft hackle of gray. Using brown hackle fore and aft is credited to Harris E. "Bob" Streety of Mesa, Arizona. It is an excellent pattern in Mexican Hay as well as at Becker, Crescent, and Big lakes.

Hook: Mustad 79580, 4X or 3665A, 6X.
Hook Size: 10 to 16.
Thread: Dark olive 6/0.
Body: Peacock herl, wrapped with tying thread.
Hackle: Brown saddle, fore and aft.
Head: Tying thread.
Source: John McKim, 1982.

Chaddock (wet)

This pattern originated in Canada. It is a good producer in the spring when that little flash of color and tinsel is needed. This fly appears in *Effective Lake Flies* by Mike Andreasen and Allen Ryther. I use it mostly in a size 12 at Becker, Sunrise, and Concho lakes. I tie it in olive instead of black.

Hook: Mustad 79580, 4X.
Hook Size: 6 to 14.
Thread: Olive 6/0.
Abdomen: Red yarn or dubbing.
Rear Hackle: Pheasant rump, color to match chenille, tied back wet style.
Rib: Fine silver Mylar, wrapped over the chenille thorax only.
Thorax: Medium or fine olive chenille.
Front Hackle: Pheasant rump, color to match chenille, tied back wet style.
Head: Tying thread.
Source: Mike Andreasen and Allen Ryther, 1990.

Horseshoe Cienega Lake.

Lady Power Fly (wet)

This fly is the first in a series of bead–head flies that have recently proved to be effective in windy weather when it can be difficult to get a fly down to the proper depth. It incorporates the attractor colors of the Peacock Lady the weight of a gold (brass) bead head, and the trout–catching tying style of Jack Gartside's Sparrow. This attractor pattern has been effective at Concho, Horseshoe Cienega, Earl Park, and Hulsey lakes in the White Mountains.

Hook:	Mustad 79580, 4X.
Hook Size:	8 to 12.
Head:	Gold (brass) bead.
Thread:	Black 6/0.
Tail:	Red marabou pinched off short.
Rib:	Fine oval, gold or silver tinsel.
Body:	Peacock herl wrapped with tying thread or dubbed Arizona synthetic peacock.
Hackle:	Natural colored pheasant rump feather wrapped two to four turns.
Collar:	Appropriate size brown, webbed saddle hackle tied with barbs standing up or dyed brown filoplume or brown chenille for smaller sizes.
Source:	The author, 1996.

Corn Cobb (wet)

The Corn Cobb is a good bright-day fly that will take trout during the midday doldrums of summer. In late June 1988 I took 10 rainbows from 7:00 a.m. to 12:30 p.m. All were in the 10- to 11-inch range. They were taken on a variety of my favorite patterns. It was rather hard fishing to say the least. It got harder. From 12:30 to 3:45 p.m., I went fishless. At the end of that time I tied on a Corn Cobb. I took five rainbow trout in the next 37 minutes. One of these was a fat 16-incher and another stretched the tape to 15 inches. This fly provided the excitement of the day for me. After netting the last of the five, I left the lake feeling very gratified.

    Hook: Mustad 9672, 3X.
Hook Size: 8 to 14.
  Thread: Brown 6/0.
     Tail: Red Acrylic yarn tied in a loop.
    Body: Medium, fine, or X-fine yellow chenille.
  Hackle: Brown saddle, full body palmer, tied in by the butt.
    Head: Tying thread.
  Source: Unknown.

Fire Bugger (wet)

This is an all-around pattern that has saved the day on several occasions. It is equally as good a bass fly as it is a trout-taker. It has been effective on Rainbow, Becker, Concho, Crescent, and Big lakes. It can be effective midday on a bright day and can be fished all year long. It has never produced large numbers of trout on any given day. It has, however, kept me from getting blanked on more than one occasion.

    Hook: Mustad 3665A, 6X or 79580, 4X.
Hook Size: 8 to 14.
  Thread: Orange 6/0.
     Tail: Orange marabou.
    Body: Fine or X-fine orange chenille.
  Hackle: Brown saddle, full body palmer, tied in by the tip.
    Head: Tying thread.
  Source: The author, 1987.

Newcommer (wet)

This is another of the short-tailed Buggers. The jury is still out on this pattern. It has showed real promise in the few times it was used in the latter months of 1995. It produces when some of the other flies of this type do not. The brown trout in Christmas Tree Lake have found this fly to their liking.

Hook:	Mustad 9671, 2X.
Hook Size:	8 to 14.
Thread:	Black 6/0.
Tail:	Light olive marabou (short), pinched off (not cut), about the length of the body.
Hackle:	Black saddle, tied in by the butt.
Body:	Medium, fine, X-fine, light olive chenille.
Head:	Tying thread.
Source:	The author, 1995.

Allen's Montana Nymph (wet)

This fly showed up in one of our local fly shops some years ago and White Mountain summer resident Ted Allen purchased some. The fly shop changed hands and the fly was gone. It is available in the 1996 Orvis fly fishing catalog. I have tied a number of these for Ted over the past several years. He has a high confidence level in this pattern and uses it often. It serves him well most of the time.

Hook:	Mustad 9672, 3X.
Hook Size:	8 to 14.
Thread:	Black 6/0 for all but the head.
Tail:	Black hackle fibers or black marabou, pinched off short.
Body:	Black chenille.
Wing Case:	Black chenille.
Thorax:	Chartreuse chenille.
Legs:	Black hackle, wound through the thorax.
Head:	Red Tying thread.
Source:	Ted Allen, 1992; Orvis, 1996.

Medium Olive Bugger (wet)

This is another of the short-tailed olive Buggers. It tends to pick up the slack when the dark and light patterns are not working well. This is one of those flies that I use when the old standbys just won't work.

Hook:	Mustad 9672, 3X.
Hook Size:	8 to 14.
Thread:	Olive 6/0.
Tail:	Medium olive marabou (short), pinched off (not cut), about the length of the body.
Body:	Medium, fine, or X-fine olive chenille.
Hackle:	Grizzly saddle, full body palmer, tied in by the butt.
Head:	Tying thread.
Source:	The author, 1986.

Dusty Teaser (wet)

The Dusty Teaser is another Woolly Worm pattern worthy of a name. It produces well at Becker, Sunrise, and Concho lakes. It is another pattern that I go to last. The brookies in Sunrise love it.

Hook:	Mustad 9672, 3X.
Hook Size:	12 to 14.
Thread:	Brown 6/0.
Body:	X-fine brown chenille.
Hackle:	Black saddle, full body palmer, tied in by the butt.
Head:	Tying thread.
Source:	The author, 1987.

Mexican Hay Lake.

Original Woolly Bugger
(wet)

What more can be said about this pattern. It is effective in both lakes and streams and could probably catch fish on a freeway. It is tied here mostly in sizes 8 through 12. This pattern is described by its originator, Russell Blessing in a fine article in the April 1989 issue of *Flyfishing* magazine.

Hook: Mustad 9672, 3X.
Hook Size: 8 to 14.
Thread: Black 6/0.
Tail: Black marabou.
Body: Medium, fine, or X-fine dark olive chenille.
Hackle: Black saddle, full body palmer, tied in by the tip.
Head: Tying thread.
Source: Russell Blessing, 1989.

Green Power Fly (wet)

This fly is another in a series of bead-head flies that have recently proved to be effective in windy weather when it can be difficult to get a fly down to the proper depth. It is tied very much the same as the Lady Power Fly. This attractor pattern has been especially effective at Concho Lake on the cutthroat population.

Hook: Mustad 79580, 4X.
Hook Size: 8 to 12.
Head: Gold (brass) bead.
Thread: Black 6/0.
Tail: Kelly Green (not olive) marabou pinched off (not cut) short.
Rib: Fine oval, gold or silver tinsel.
Body: Fine or X-fine Kelly green chenille.
Hackle: Natural-colored pheasant rump feather wrapped two to four turns.
Collar: Appropriate size dyed green, webbed saddle hackle tied with barbs standing up or dyed green filoplume or green chenille for smaller sizes.
Source: The author, 1997.

Salt And Pepper Teaser (wet)

This was my number–one fly for fishing Mexican Hay Lake. When fished slow and deep with a sink–tip line, it can be deadly. Mexican Hay Lake did not give up its secrets easily. This was one I discovered through a long trial–and–error process. It is also effective in Sunrise and Concho lakes.

Hook: Mustad 9672, 3X.
Hook Size: 10 to 16.
Thread: Black 6/0.
Body: Fine or X–fine black chenille.
Hackle: Grizzly saddle, full body palmer, tied in by the butt.
Head: Tying thread.
Source: Unknown.

Brown Teaser (wet)

This is another case of trying to give a lowly Woolly Worm pattern a little status. This pattern works everywhere and nowhere. It is not a pattern that I use normally as a starter on any given day. It is one that I end up with when all the "hot" patterns have let me down. When tied with a red tail, it is known as the Becker Lake Special .

Hook: Mustad 9672, 3X.
Hook Size: 10 to 16.
Thread: Brown 6/0.
Body: Fine or X–fine chenille.
Hackle: Brown saddle, full body palmer, tied in by the butt.
Head: Tying thread.
Source: Unknown.

Brown Blazetail (wet)

This fly is similar to the Becker Lake Special except that it has a longer tail of orange marabou. This pattern has worked very well in Big, Crescent, and Cyclone lakes.

Hook: Mustad 9672, 3X.
Hook Size: 8 to 16.

Thread: Brown 6/0.
   Tail: Orange marabou (short), pinched off (not cut), about the length of the body.
  Body: Medium, fine, or X–fine brown chenille.
Hackle: Brown saddle, full body palmer, tied in by the butt.
  Head: Tying thread.
Source: Unknown.

White Doll Fly (wet)

Another simple pattern to tie, this fly is especially good at Becker Lake in the late after-noon in the spring, summer, or fall. It is also a very good warm–water lake fly for crap-pies and smallmouth bass.

     Hook: Mustad 9672, 3X.
Hook Size: 2 to 14.
   Thread: White 6/0.
     Tail: White marabou (short), pinched off (not cut), about the length of the body.
    Body: Fine, X–fine white chenille.
  Collar: Badger saddle, tied back wet style.
    Head: Tying thread.
  Source: The author, 1986.

Dark Olive Eyebug (wet)

This is another of the Eyefly series. It is a good alternate pattern when others are not working. It is an effective pat-tern to use in those lakes where damsel nymphs are darker in color than the usual light olive.

     Hook: Mustad 79580, 4X.
Hook Size: 12 to 14.
   Thread: Black or dark olive 6/0.
     Tail: Black marabou (short), pinched off (not cut), 1/3 to 1/2 the length of the body.
    Body: X–fine dark olive chenille.
  Hackle: Grizzly saddle, palmer the front 1/3 of body, tied in by the butt.
    Head: Tying thread.
    Eyes: Black, 2mm.
  Source: The author, 1992.

Pearl Ribbed Shiner (wet)

First cousin to the Shiner, this fly is also a good producer. It has a pearlescent rib that is suggestive of the white or light colored banding on some midge pupae. The Ribbed Shiner is especially productive in the spring. It works well in Concho Lake.

Hook:	Mustad 79580, 3X.
Hook Size:	12 to 14.
Thread:	Black 6/0.
Tail:	Black marabou (short), pinched off (not cut), 1/3 to 1/2 the length of the body.
Body:	X-fine black chenille.
Rib:	Pearlescent punch yarn or Flashabou.
Hackle:	Grizzly saddle, palmer the front 1/3 of body, tied in by the butt.
Head:	Tying thread.
Eyes:	Black, 2mm.
Source:	The author, 1992.

Jack Kennedy (wet)

Jack Kennedy was one of the men who fished Christmas Tree Lake on May 28, 1995. He has had great success with this light olive, damsel nymph sim-ulator. He has not only done well at Christmas Tree Lake but also a number of other lakes as well. Jack mostly trolls and catches and releases many fish

throughout the summer. A short-bodied version of this fly brought the author a 22-inch rainbow at Concho Lake on April 9, 1992.

Hook:	Mustad 79580, 4X.
Hook Size:	12 to 14.
Thread:	Olive 6/0.
Tail:	Light olive marabou (short), pinched off (not cut), 1/2 to 3/4 the length of the body.
Body:	X-fine, light olive chenille.
Hackle:	Grizzly saddle, palmer the front 1/3 of the body, tied in by the butt.
Head:	Tying thread.
Eyes:	Black, 2mm.
Source:	The author, 1992.

Gold Body Hair-Winged Streamer (wet)

This pattern works very well at Big Lake, Crescent, Sunrise, and other of the higher lakes that have brook trout in them. It is also a good trolling fly for rainbow trout in all the lakes. It is a simple and sparsely tied minnow simulator that is a producer. It is especially good in the spring or early summer when minnows are producing spawn.

Hook: Mustad 3665A, 6X or 79580, 4X.
Hook Size: 12 to 14.
Thread: Black 6/0.
Body: Gold Mylar tubing.
Wing: Gray squirrel tail.
Head: Tying thread.
Source: Unknown.

Kelly Green Bugger (wet)

This pattern is a spinoff from the KP Bugger and again the result of more experimentation. If a green body worked, why not try a green tail too. Add grizzly hackle instead of black and "voilá" the Kelly Green was born. It also helped to have a number of good lakes nearby to test this critter. In its first season it made my top 24 list.

Hook: Mustad 9672, 3X.
Hook Size: 8 to 14.
Thread: Green 6/0.
Tail: Kelly green marabou (short), pinched off (not cut), about the length of the body.
Body: Medium, fine, X–fine Kelly green chenille.
Hackle: Grizzly saddle, full body palmer, tied in by the butt.
Head: Tying thread.
Source: The author, 1993.

Becker Lake.

KP Bugger Light (wet)

Another of the short-tailed Buggers this one is tied with medium-green chenille. It was tried for the first time in 1995 and worked very well for the few times it was used.

Hook:	Mustad 9672, 3X.
Hook Size:	8 to 14.
Thread:	Black 6/0.
Tail:	Black marabou (short), pinched off (not cut), about the length of the body.
Body:	Medium, fine, X-fine medium-green chenille.
Hackle:	Black saddle, full body palmer, tied in by the butt.
Head:	Tying thread.
Source:	The author, 1995.

Salt & Pepper Bugger (wet)

This was another very good pattern for Mexican Hay Lake. It still continues to produce in Crescent Lake.

Hook:	Mustad 9672, 3X.
Hook Size:	10 to 16.
Thread:	Black 6/0.
Tail:	Black marabou (short), pinched off (not cut), about the length of the body.
Body:	Fine or X-fine black chenille.
Hackle:	Grizzly saddle, full body palmer, tied in by the butt.
Head:	Tying thread.
Source:	Unknown.

Bigg's Special (wet)

This fly amazes me with its fish–catching powers. To me it doesn't look like anything that I would associate with the insect world. It apparently has a different effect on trout populations and must look like an ice cream sundae to them. I have had vicious strikes at Stone Lake in New Mexico with the Bigg's. It also has been effective closer to home at Becker Lake.

> *Hook*: Mustad 79580, 4X.
> *Hook Size*: 8 to 14.
> *Thread*: Black 6/0.
> *Tail*: No tail; tie in aft brown saddle hackle and wrap three turns and tie off.
> *Body*: Dark peacock or light olive chenille.
> *Wing*: A pinch of well–barred mallard flank (20–25 fibers). Tie in at head and extend to just short of the aft hackle.
> *Source*: Mike Andreasen and Allen Ryther, 1990.

Bead-Head Sparrow, Light Olive (wet)

This is another bead–head fly tied in the style of the Lady Power Fly and the Green Power Fly. This fly has consistently produced at Earl Park Lake when all else has failed. It is most effective in windy weather when fished very slow and very deep.

> *Hook*: Mustad 79580, 4X.
> *Hook Size*: 8 to 12.
> *Head*: Gold (brass) bead
> *Thread*: Olive 6/0.
> *Tail*: Light olive (not green) marabou pinched off (not cut) short.
> *Body*: Dubbed olive Hare–Tron.
> *Hackle*: Olive–dyed pheasant rump feather wrapped two to four turns.
> *Collar*: Olive–dyed filoplume.
> *Source*: The author, 1996.

Yeager Damsel (wet)

This pattern is tied the same as the Jack Kennedy fly with the addition of a pinch of marabou on either side of the body. The addition of the marabou adds to the movement of the fly when retrieved. It has produced trout up to 21 inches at Stone Lake. It has also been effective at Earl Park Lake.

  Hook: Mustad 79580, 4X.
Hook Size: 12 to 14.
 Thread: Olive 6/0.
  Tail: Light olive marabou (short), pinched off (not cut), 1/2 to 3/4 the length of the body.
 Body: X–fine olive chenille.
Side Wings: A small pinch of light olive marabou tied in on either side of body, extending to the end of the body.
 Hackle: Grizzly saddle, palmer the front 1/3 of the body, tied in by the butt.
 Head: Tying thread.
 Eyes: Black, 2mm.
Source: The author, 1996.

Bird's Nest (wet)

This pattern shows great potential as a lake fly. I have used it almost exclusively at Earl Park Lake. It has saved the day several times when all the normally good flies failed.

  Hook: Mustad 9671, 2X.
Hook Size: 10 to 16.
 Thread: Black 6/0.
  Tail: Webbed grizzly hackle fibers or small pinch of chickabou no longer than the body.
Abdomen: Dark olive dubbing.
 Legs: Same as tail extending beyond hook bend.
 Thorax: Same as abdomen.
Source: Randall Kaufmann, 1994.

River Reservoir.

Ribless Zulu (wet)

This pattern will produce moderate action in most of the White Mountain lakes. It's always a good idea to have a supply of these in several sizes for use when all the old standbys fail. This pattern is very similar to the Zulu illustrated in *Effective Lake Flies*, by Mike Andreasen and Allen Ryther, 1990. Terry Hellekson writes this fly up without a rib and with a peacock herl body in *Popular Fly Patterns*, 1984 and *Fish Flies Volume I*, 1995. The differences in this pattern and those already written about, are that the hackle is tied in by the butt and palmered sparsely. The pattern is not ribbed and black chenille is used for the body.

      Hook: Mustad 9671, 2X.
Hook Size: 12 to 14.
   Thread: Black 6/0.
      Tail: Red acrylic yarn.
     Body: Fine or X–fine black chenille.
   Hackle: Black saddle, full body palmer, tied in by the butt.
     Head: Tying thread.
   Source: Mike Andreasen and Allen Ryther, 1990; Terry Hellekson, 1984, 1995.

Bird's Eye (wet)

This is another member of the Eyefly series. It is an alternative version of the Shiner. It allows a slight color variation that may be needed at times to move large trout.

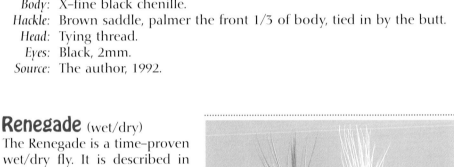

    Hook: Mustad 79580, 4X.
Hook Size: 12 to 14.
  Thread: Black 6/0.
    Tail: Black marabou
        (short), pinched off (not cut), 1/3 to 1/2 the length of the body.
   Body: X–fine black chenille.
 Hackle: Brown saddle, palmer the front 1/3 of body, tied in by the butt.
  Head: Tying thread.
  Eyes: Black, 2mm.
Source: The author, 1992.

Renegade (wet/dry)

The Renegade is a time–proven wet/dry fly. It is described in about every fly-tying pattern book currently in print. An article in the fall 1983 issue of *Fly Tyer* written by Dave McCracken is undecided as to how this fly originated. It may have come to us via "Beartracks" Williams a pipeline

worker in Wyoming in 1928 or it was imported from England in the name of George Selwyn Marryat. Marryat was born at Winchester England in 1840. Mrs. Edith Cox reportedly first tied the fly for Marryat and named it the Marryat for him. Over the years, many versions of this popular fly have developed. The one illustrated is the one most commonly used, both wet and dry, by the author.

      Hook: Mustad 94840, 1X or 7957B, 1X.
  Hook Size: 6 to 18.
    Thread: Black 6/0.
      Tip: Flat gold tinsel.
Rear Hackle: Brown, neck or saddle for dry or wet tie.
     Body: Peacock herl, reverse wrapped with fine gold wire.
Front Hackle: White, neck or saddle for dry or wet tie.
   Head: Tying thread.
 Source: Dave McCracken, 1983.

Scud or Freshwater Shrimp (wet)

Two genera (*Gammarus* and *Hyalella*) of scuds or freshwater shrimp are found in various White Mountain lakes. Neither are found in all lakes. *Hyalella*, the very small scud, is common to Becker, Concho, Mexican Hay, Rainbow, and Sunrise lakes. *Gammarus*, the larger of the species, does not appear to be as widely spread as is its smaller cousin. Sunrise Lake is one of the few local waters where the author has found this larger species. Where scuds are found they usually occur by the millions. They are an important part of the food base for trout in those waters where they abound. Scuds swim freely, primarily at night and on dark cloudy days. They seek the shelter and security of aquatic vegetation during bright or sunlit days. Scud patterns can be dynamite on cloudy days and also in the early morning and late afternoon.

Hook: Mustad 7957B, 1X.
Hook Size: 8 to 16.
Thread: Black, brown, or olive 6/0.
Tail: Brown hackle fibers, tied short.
Body: Black, brown, or olive Antron dubbing.
Wing Case: Clear plastic film, used for shellback.
Rib: Fine copper wire.
Legs: Pick out dubbing under the body.
Head: Tying thread.
Source: Randall Kaufmann, 1975.

Concho Lake.

Red Rooster (wet)

This pattern is another of my experimental contrivances. I was looking for another use for the russet brown breast feathers of a ring–necked pheasant cock and came up with this. At times it is a real trout worrier.

Hook:	Mustad 9672, 3X.
Hook Size:	8 to 14.
Thread:	Brown 6/0.
Tail:	None.
Rear Hackle:	Russet brown breast feather from a ring–necked pheasant.
Body:	Filoplume, loop dubbed.
Front Hackle:	Russet brown breast feather from a ring–necked pheasant.
Head:	Tying thread.
Source:	The author, 1987.

Black Martinez (wet)

The late Don Martinez was credited with opening the first fly shop in the West Yellowstone area in the 1930s. He was a great innovator as a fly tier. He created a number of patterns that were quite successful. The Black Martinez is an example of that creativity. It has become a standard pattern throughout North America. It was created primarily for river/stream fishing but has adaptability to lake fishing. It has been an excellent substitute for the Salt and Pepper Teaser at Mexican Hay Lake. It has also works well at Sunrise Lake.

Hook:	Mustad 9671, 2X.
Hook Size:	8 to 12.
Thread:	Black 6/0.
Tail:	Speckled guinea fibers.
Rib:	Fine oval gold tinsel.
Body:	Dubbed black muskrat fur, body should be picked out and made shaggy.
Thorax:	Black chenille.
Wing Case:	Green raffia, tied in over the thorax.
Hackle:	Gray partridge, tied full and back wet style.
Head:	Tying thread.
Source:	Terry Hellekson, 1984.

Big Lake.

Grizzly Ugly (wet)

This is a pattern that Kirk asked me to tie for him to use at Sunrise Lake. It works there and at most other lakes. It is an effectively ugly fly.

　　　　Hook: Mustad 3906B, 1X.
　Hook Size: 8 to 14.
　　Thread: Black 6/0.
Rear Hackle: Grizzly, saddle.
　　　Body: Black ostrich herl.
Front Hackle: Grizzly, saddle.
　　　Head: Tying thread.
　　Source: Bob Kirkpatrick and the author, 1988.

Big Lake Special (wet)

A friend of mine in Yuma, Arizona gave this pattern to me. It is a very durable and productive fly. It is also very inexpensive to tie.

　　　　　Hook: Mustad 9672, 3X.
　　 Hook Size: 8 to 14.
　　　 Thread: Brown 6/0.
　　　　 Tail: None.
　　 Abdomen: Burlap.
Abdomen Hackle: Brown saddle.
　　　 Thorax: Burlap.
 Thorax Hackle: Brown saddle.
　　　　 Head: Tying thread.
　　　Source: Larry Voyles, 1990.

Elk Hair Caddis (dry)

This pattern continues its pop-ularity all over the West and beyond as a stream pattern. It was originated by Al Troth and reemphasized by Eric Leiser in his publication *The Book Of Fly Patterns*. It is always a good lake pattern in the high country when trout are feeding on the surface. It has produced very well for me in Lee Valley Lake at approximately 9400 feet elevation.

      Hook: Mustad 94840, Std.
Hook Size: 10 to 20.
   Thread: Tan or brown 6/0.
     Body: Hare's ear and mask dubbing fur.
    Wings: Tan colored elk body hair.
   Hackle: Brown or furnace, full body palmer, tied in by the butt, dry-fly quality.
     Head: Tying thread.
   Source: Eric Leiser, 1987.

Royal Wulff (dry)

Another of the old guard, when-in-doubt patterns. Although created primarily as a fly for use on rivers and streams it also has application for lake fishing. The Royal Wulff can be used on all lakes whenever surface feeding occurs. The smaller sizes 12 and 14 seem to work better than those of a larger size in our local waters. It has taken some nice native Apache trout at Christmas Tree Lake.

      Hook: Mustad 7957B, 1X.
Hook Size: 8 to 14.
   Thread: Brown 6/0.
    Wings: White calf tail or calf body hair.
     Tail: Deer, elk, or moose body hair.
     Body: Royal Coachman style, peacock herl/red floss/peacock herl.
   Hackle: Brown, neck, dry-fly quality.
     Head: Tying thread.
   Source: Terry Hellekson, 1984.

Trueblood Shrimp Brown (wet)

This is a combination scud/nymph type pattern. One of these in a size 12 took a nice 17-inch brown trout at Becker Lake on November 10, 1986. These can be tied in several colors as described in Randall Kaufmann's *Tying Nymphs*. This pattern is sometimes referred to as the Otter Nymph.

    Hook: Mustad 3906, Std or 3906B, 1X.
Hook Size: 8 to 16.
  Thread: Brown, or to match dubbed body, 6/0.
    Body: Dubbed otter and cream Angora goat, mixed 50/50 or sand-colored Antron.
    Legs: Brown partridge fibers, tied in at the throat.
    Head: Tying thread.
  Source: Randall Kaufmann, 1994.

Yellow Doll Fly (wet)

Whether used for trout or crappie, this fly works. After having not fished Becker Lake for some five years (the lake was drained in 1989) I decided to take a chance and went back there on May 3, 1994. It was sunny but very windy. Nine trout were taken that day. The largest was a 19-inch rainbow taken on (you guessed it) a size 10 Yellow Doll Fly. Another bright-day fly that is also a trip-saver.

    Hook: Mustad 9672, 3X.
Hook Size: 8 to 16.
  Thread: Yellow 6/0.
    Tail: Yellow marabou.
    Body: Yellow chenille.
  Hackle: Badger saddle, tied back wet style.
    Head: Tying thread.
  Source: The author, 1986.

Floating Ant (dry)

Winged termites appear often in the White Mountains. They respond to temperature and humidity and swarm in an effort to establish new colonies. Oftentimes the swarming is in association with summer thunderstorms. The very strong winds that accompany those storms carry the swarming insects in whatever direction it happens to be blowing. Hundreds of these insects can be deposited on a lake surface in just a few minutes. When this happens, trout can come unglued and start a voracious feeding frenzy. The floating ant pattern is a very effective terrestrial when the "ants" hit the water. Several sizes from 12 to 18 should be carried in both red and black.

  Hook: Mustad 94840, Std.
Hook Size: 2 to 16.
  Thread: Black 6/0.
  Body: Black, McMurray balsa wood or poly foam cylinder.
  Hackle: Black neck, tied in at mid–body (waist).
  Head: Tying thread.
  Source: Eric Leiser, 1987.

Wade Walker Special

(wet)

This is another Woolly Worm type pattern. Kirk introduced it to me several years ago when we fished Luna Lake together. He said that it was originated by a local fisherman of the same name. It still works at Luna Lake on both rainbow and brook trout. It has also taken its toll at Concho Lake.

  Hook: Mustad 9672, 3X.
Hook Size: 8 to 14.
  Thread: Yellow 6/0.
  Body: Yellow floss.
  Hackle: Grizzly saddle, full body palmer, tied in by the butt.
  Head: Yellow tying thread, somewhat enlarged.
  Source: Bob Kirkpatrick, 1986.

Zug Bug (wet)

The Zug Bug was one of the first patterns I learned to tie after I mastered the Woolly Worm. It met with immediate success on Concho Lake mid–March 1986. The Zug Bug helped me to my first ever 30+ fish day as a fly fisher. I took 31 rainbow trout that day. It is a good pattern

wherever midge pupae make up a substantial portion of the food base. This generally includes all of the fishable lakes in the White Mountains.

> *Hook:* Mustad 3906B, 1X.
> *Hook Size:* 8 to 16.
> *Thread:* Black 6/0.
> *Tail:* Three to six peacock sword fibers.
> *Body:* Peacock herl, wrapped with tying thread.
> *Rib:* Flat or oval, gold or silver tinsel.
> *Wing Case:* Mallard dyed wood duck, 1/3 the body length.
> *Hackle:* Brown saddle, full collar or beard.
> *Head:* Tying thread.
> *Source:* Randall Kaufmann, 1975.

Picket Pin (wet)

Brad Coen, a former branch manager of First Interstate Bank in Show Low, Arizona, introduced this fly to me prior to his moving to the Phoenix area. He was president of the White Mountain Fly–casters Association at the time. Unfortunately, as of this

writing, neither the club nor Brad is in the area any longer. The Picket Pin, however, continues on and has proven to be a consistent producer of trout in the White Mountains.

> *Hook:* Mustad 9671, 2X.
> *Hook Size:* 4 to 10.
> *Thread:* Black 3/0 or 6/0, (depending on hook size).
> *Tail:* Golden pheasant tippet barbs.
> *Body:* Peacock herl, wrapped with tying thread.
> *Wings:* Tan elk body hair topped with red fox squirrel tail.
> *Hackle:* Brown, saddle.
> *Head:* Peacock herl.
> *Source:* Jack Dennis, 1980.

Zonker (wet)

This pattern is described in Eric Leiser's *The Book of Fly Patterns*. It was originated by Dan Byford. This is an excellent baitfish simulator for casting or trolling. Most of the local high-country lakes have some type of minnow population (fathead and/or golden shiners). All local

trout species will prey on minnows at virtually all times of the year.

Hook:	Mustad 9674, 4X.
Hook Size:	2 to 8.
Thread:	Black and red 3/0 or 6/0.
Underbody:	Trimbrite, metallic tape.
Body:	Mylar tubing.
Butt/Tag:	Red thread, to tie the rabbit wing down.
Hackle:	Grizzly saddle, tied as wet-fly color.
Wing:	A tanned strip of natural brown/gray rabbit fur on skin.
Head:	Tying thread.
Source:	Eric Leiser, 1987.

Muddler Minnow
(Wet/Dry)

This fly was Don Gapen's legacy to the fly fishermen of the world. It is arguably the best fly ever tied for fishing (Woolly Bugger notwithstanding). I have seen this fly work its magic at Becker Lake when retrieved very slowly in deep water.

Hook:	Mustad 79580, 4X.
Hook Size:	2 to 12.
Thread:	Gray or brown, A, 3/0 or 6/0.
Tail:	Mottled turkey wing quill.
Body:	Flat gold tinsel.
Underwing:	Gray squirrel tail.
Overwing:	Two mottled turkey wing quills.
Hackle:	Spun deer hair.
Head:	Spun deer hair, clipped to a bullet shape.
Source:	Eric Leiser, 1987.

Tom Knight (wet)

I originally dubbed this pattern the "Concho Killer" because of its ability to take trout in Concho Lake. I later renamed the pattern after Tom Knight, a longtime, avid stream-fisher who climbed into a float tube for the first time at the age of 79. The fact that this fly takes trout is indisputable to me. It has been successful at Stone Lake and in the San Juan River in New Mexico. This series of olive Buggers (Yeagerburger, Medium Olive Bugger, Tom Knight, and Newcommer), are very good lake flies. These simulator patterns work exceptionally well in lakes where there are good populations of snails, damselfly nymphs, and dragonfly nymphs.

Hook:	Mustad 9672, 3X.
Hook Size:	8 to 14.
Thread:	Olive 6/0.
Tail:	Light olive marabou (short), pinched off (not cut), about the length of the body.
Body:	Medium, fine, X-fine olive chenille.
Hackle:	Grizzly saddle, full body palmer, tied in by the butt.
Head:	Tying thread.
Source:	The author, 1986.

KP Bugger-Dark (wet)

This is a most effective pattern in the White Mountains. Kirk liked it so well that I dubbed it the KP Bugger. In a size 12 it has produced a number of 30+ fish days since first using it in 1989. It is a great evening fly at Stone Lake. This pattern in a size 8 has proved to be an excellent fly for trolling. As usual, the fly is not weighted.

Hook:	Mustad 9672, 3X.
Hook Size:	8 to 14.
Thread:	Black 6/0.
Tail:	Black marabou (short), pinched off (not cut), about the length of the body.
Body:	Medium, fine X-fine Kelly green chenille.
Hackle:	Black saddle, full body palmer, tied in by the butt.
Head:	Tying thread.
Source:	The author, 1988.

FLY INDEX

BIBLIOGRAPHY

Alley, Robert. *Advanced Lake Fly Fishing: The Skillful Tuber.* Portland, Oregon: Frank Amato Publications, 1991.
Andreasen, Mike and A. Ryther. *Effective Lake Flies.* West Jordan, Utah: Allami Publications, 1991.
Blessing, Russell. *Flyfishing.* "The Birth of the Bugger." April, 1989. Vol. 12 No. 1. Frank Amato Publications.
Cordes, Ron and Randall Kaufmann. *Lake Fishing With A Fly.* Portland, Oregon: Frank Amato Publications, 1984.
Dennis, Jack. *Western Trout Fly Tying Manual.* Jackson Hole, Wyoming: Snake River Books, 1974.
Dennis, Jack. *Western Trout Fly Tying Manual. Vol. 2.* Jackson Hole, Wyoming: Snake River Books, 1980.
Fling, Paul N. and D. L. Puterbaugh. *The Basic Manual Of Fly-Tying.* New York: Sterling Publishing Co., Inc. 1981.
Fling, Paul N. and D. L. Puterbaugh. *Expert Fly-Tying.* New York, New York: Sterling Publishing Co., Inc. 1982.
Harris, Bob. *American Fly Tyer.* "Sparrow and Parson's Glory." Summer 1986. Vol. 9, No. 1. Northland Press, Intervale, N.H. 1986.
Hellekson, Terry. *Popular Fly Patterns.* Salt Lake City: Peregrine Smith Books, 1984.
Kaufmann, Randall. *American Nymph Fly Tying Manual.* Portland, Oregon: Frank Amato Publications, 1975.
Kaufmann, Randall. *Tying Nymphs.* Portland, Oregon: Western Fisherman's Press, 1994.
Leiser, Eric. *The Complete Book Of Fly Tying.* New York, New York: Alfred Knopf, 1983.
Leiser, Eric. *The Book Of Fly Patterns.* New York, New York: Alfred Knopf, 1987.
Lilly, Bud and P. Schullery. *Bud Lilly's Guide to Western Fly Fishing.* New York, New York: Nick Lyons Books, 1987.
McCracken, Dave. *Fly Tyer.* "Renegade and Bear Paw, Fore & Aft Flies." Fall 1983. Vol. 6, No. 3. Fly Tyer Inc., North Conway, NH. 1983.
McKim, John. *Fly Tying: Adventures In Fur, Feathers And Fun.* Missoula, Montana: Mountain Press Publishing Co., 1982.
Merwin, John (editor). *Stillwater Trout.* New York, New York: Nick Lyons Books, 1980.
Meyer, Deke. *Float Tube Fly Fishing.* Portland, Oregon: Frank Amato Publications, 1989.
Nelson, David L. (editor) *Patterns of the Masters.* West Yellowstone, Montana: Federation of Fly Fishers Conclave, 1991.
Probasco, Steve. *American Angler & Fly Tyer.* "Short Buggers." Winter 1988. Northland Press, 1988.
Roberts, Don. *Nymph Fishing Lakes.* Portland, Oregon: Frank Amato Publications, 1978.
Rogers, Tim. *Flyfishing.* "Multiple Anchors For Stillwater Fly Fishing." May/June, 1995. Portland, Oregon. Frank Amato Publications, 1995.
Rosborough, E.H. "Polly". *Fly Tyer.* "Debunking A Few Myths & Fantasies." Fly Tyer Inc., Spring 1985.
Ruttner, Franz. *Fundamentals of Limnology.* Toronto, Canada: University of Toronto Press, 1953.
Schullery, Paul. *American Angler* "Comfort for the Leader Impaired." Intervale, New Hampshire: Northland Press, Inc., May-June, 1991.
Surett, Dick (editor). *Fly Tyer Pattern Bible.* North Conway, New Hampshire: Saco River Publishing Corp, 1985.